T0197392

What It Takes to Cut a Walnut Tree

Brittany S. Knox

To order additional copies of this book, contact:
Xlibris
844-714-8691
www.Xlibris.com
Orders@Xlibris.com

ISBN: Softcover   979-8-3694-1326-5
        EBook   979-8-3694-1325-8

Library of Congress Control Number: 2023923895

Print information available on the last page

Rev. date: 12/19/2023

What It Takes to Cut a Walnut Tree

The logger will talk to people with farms and land to see if the walnut trees are big enough to cut down.

The perfect walnut tree is sixteen inches in diameter. This is called a veneer log. A veneer log will be smooth with no holes.

The smallest walnut tree that you would want would have a ten-inch diameter and be at least eight feet tall.

The logger will walk the property with the landowner to discuss what trees to cut and determine the value of the trees.

The logger will then go through and mark what trees will be cut down.

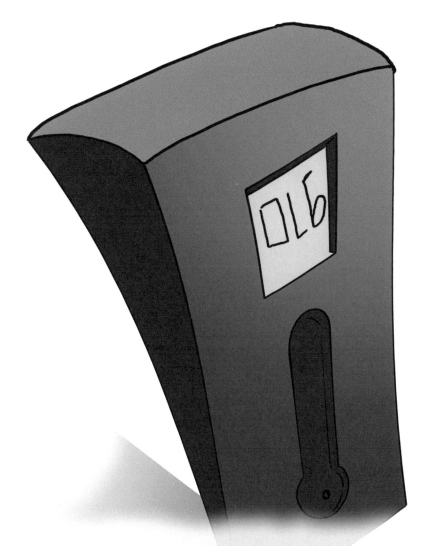

The logger will then cut the trees. The logger decides what angle to cut the trees depending on what's around the trees and how close they are to other trees. The logger will use a chainsaw and a wedge to cut the trees.

Once the trees are cut and laid on the ground, the logger will cut the limbs off and top the trees.

The logger will connect chains to the trees. These chains are connected to a dozer or skidder, which will bring the trees out of the woods.

The logger will then drag the trees from the woods to the log yard.

Once the trees are at the yard, then the logger will work the trees up.

Working a tree up means measuring the tree to the length that is appropriate.

After the trees are cut, they will be laid out with room for log buyers to come through and look at them.

The logger and the buyers will decide on prices that are suitable for the trees.

Once the trees have been looked at, they will be sorted by each buyer.

Then the logger will use a knuckle boom to load the trees on a truck.

Once the semi is loaded, the logger will head off to the buyers.

After all the trees have been bought, it's time for cleanup.

The logger will go through and clean up any mess they may have made on the landowner's property by cleaning up the branches.

Once the logger cleans up the property, the landowner and logger will go through the land and make sure the logger cleaned up properly and didn't miss any trees.

Then the buyer can make furniture, flooring, gun stocks, and doors out of the walnut trees.

Printed in the United States
by Baker & Taylor Publisher Services